NOSTRADAMUS

NOSTRADAMUS

AN ILLUSTRATED GUIDE TO HIS PREDICTIONS

Millie Ridge

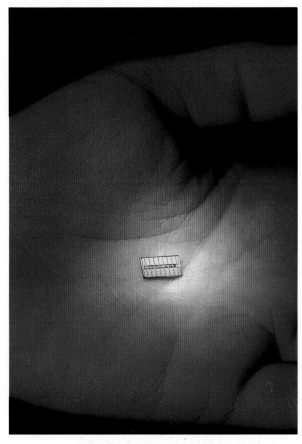

SMITHMARK

This edition published in 1993
by SMITHMARK Publishers Inc.,
16 East 32nd Street
New York, New York 10016.

SMITHMARK books are available for bulk
purchase for sales promotion and premium use.
For details write or telephone the Manager of
Special Sales, SMITHMARK Publishers Inc., 16
East 32nd Street, New York, NY 10016. (212)
532-6600.

Produced by Brompton Books Corp.,
15 Sherwood Place,
Greenwich, CT 06830.

ISBN 0-8317-6447-3

Printed in Hong Kong

10 9 8 7 6 5 4 3 2 1

CONTENTS

The right of Millie Ridge to be identified as the
author has been asserted by the same in
accordance with the Copyright, Designs and
Patents Act 1988.

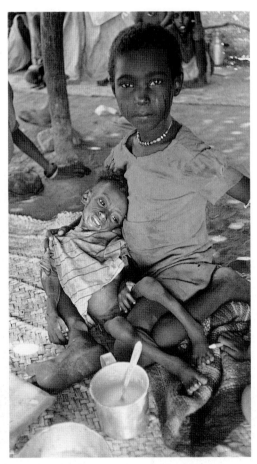

PAGE 1: *A
sixteenth-century
portrait
Nostradamus.*

PAGES 2-3:
*Nostradamus as a
young man.*

THESE PAGES: *The
plagues of the
twentieth century.*

INTRODUCTION

It seems incredible that the sophisticated inhabitants of the twentieth century should pay attention to the cryptic predictions of a man who lived in an age far more superstitious than ours. The lure of the prophecies of Nostradamus is simple: human beings have an intense curiosity about the future and Nostradamus's predictions seem more detailed than most. As long as one accepts that they genuinely were written in the sixteenth century, and that they have not subsequently been tampered with, there are many prophecies that appear to have been fulfilled. The language of the verses is complex, but not unintelligible, and some of them even include precise dates. For the curious and credulous, therefore, Nostradamus provides a satisfying view of the past, and an intriguing glimpse of the future.

Michel de Nostradame was a French physician and seer who lived in the sixteenth century. Born in 1503, he came from a Provençal family of Jewish descent and was the eldest of four sons. He was an intelligent child who received a thorough education from his grandfathers and was sent to Montpellier in 1522 to study medicine. In the course of his studies he came across astrological, astronomical and magical books and treatises and it is evident that he was not only interested in such subjects, but was also clairvoyant. He lived in a time when such interests and accomplishments were regarded with deep suspicion by the omnipresent authorities of the Catholic Church, but with fascination and awe by the populus.

Nostradamus received his license to practise medicine in 1525 and immediately set out to use his talent, helping plague victims in the south of France. He was known for his unorthodox remedies which were regarded with suspicion by many of his colleagues, but his refusal to bleed already weakened patients and an insistence on fresh air and running water ensured that his cure rate was undoubtedly higher than most. He returned to Montpellier in 1529 to obtain his doctorate, using his practical experience as the basis for his examinations.

He worked for a short time in the faculty at Montpellier, but resented the strictures imposed by the authorities, and left in about 1532. His reputation as a scholar and unorthodox physician was widening: he received a letter from Jules César Scaliger, an abrasive man, and an intellectual with a reputation second only to that of Erasmus, who enquired whether the man lived up to his name. Nostradamus met Scaliger in Agen, and found his friendship so stimulating that he decided to settle there.

He married in this period, but his wife and young family died of the plague in

LEFT: *A contemporary portrait of Nostradamus clutching some of the tools of his trade – a telescope, a globe and a pair of compasses. He is dressed in the sober black academic robes of a sixteenth-century doctor.*

BELOW: *A nineteenth-century painting by Louis Denis-Valverane showing Nostradamus examining one of the younger Valois sons in 1564.*

1534. Nostradamus quarreled with Scaliger and the two events prompted him to leave Agen and travel throughout southern Europe. For eight years he wandered through Italy and south-eastern France. He met apothecaries and physicians wherever he went, many of whom dabbled in magic, and it is at this stage that tales of his clairvoyance begin. When he was in Italy an unremarkable and poor young monk named Felix Peretti approached Nostradamus, who immediately fell to his knees. When asked why, Nostradamas replied that he knelt before His Holiness, a remark which amused his companions. In the fullness of time, however, the monk became a cardinal and, in 1585, Felix Peretti became Pope Sixtus V.

By 1544 he was back in France, working as a doctor in Marseille where the plague was endemic. Once again, he was moderately successful and, unlike many of his colleagues, managed to ensure that a large proportion of his patients survived the deadly scourge. News of his success spread, and other towns begged for his

ABOVE: *A woodblock by Hans Holbein the Younger showing the medieval view of the earth and heavens. The planets and sun clearly revolve around the earth.*

RIGHT: *The reputation of Nostradamus'* Prophecies *quickly spread throughout Europe. This is the introduction from a German edition published in 1572.*

FAR RIGHT: *The frontispiece from an early edition of the* Prophecies.

services; over the next couple of years he worked in Aix-en-Provence, Salon and Lyon. In 1547 he married a rich widow and settled in Salon where he continued his medical practice; at the same time he began his magical studies in earnest.

From 1550 onwards he produced an annual almanac of predictions for the forthcoming year, which evidently impressed his readers and encouraged him to publish the first part of the *Prophecies* in 1555. His reputation as a seer spread way beyond Provence to Paris, and the royal family. Catherine de Medici, the wife of King Henri II, was an extraordinarily superstitious woman who was understandably curious about the prophecies that apparently related to her family. Probably the most notorious prediction was one in which Nostradamus foresaw the death of the king in a joust (I:35). Nostradamus was summoned to Paris in

LEFT: *An anonymous drawing of Henri II, king of France from 1547 until his death in a tournament in 1559. Henri was well known for his love of jousts, and when the first part of the* Prophecies *was published in 1555, readers immediately noticed quatrain I:35, which predicted the king's death on the 'war-like field in single combat.'*

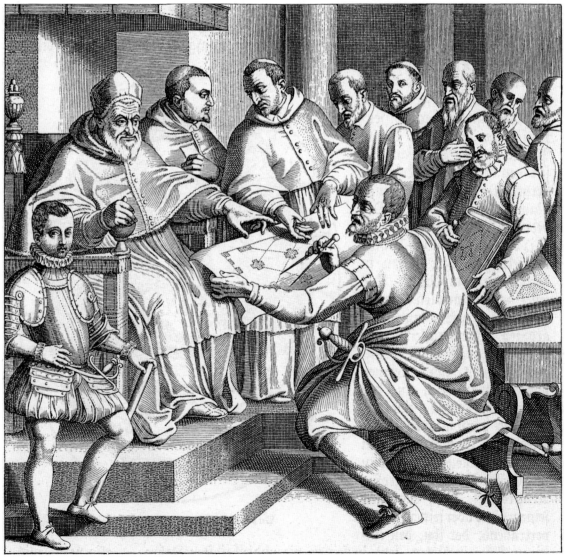

LEFT: *Pope Sixtus V, formerly the humble monk Felix Peretti. Nostradamus met him in the 1530s and predicted great things for the apparently unremarkable young man. Felix became pope in 1585.*

ABOVE: *The marriage of Catherine de Medici and Henri Valois, heir to the French throne, in 1533. Notoriously superstitious, Catherine consulted many astrologers and seers in an attempt to peer into the future. In 1556 Catherine asked Nostradamus to draw up horoscopes for her children. He predicted that four of them would be kings.*

ABOVE RIGHT AND RIGHT: *Catherine de Medici's eldest son Francis II (above right), married Mary, Queen of Scots, (right) in 1558.*

1556, met both the king and the queen, cast horoscopes for the Valois children (given their short lives, one assumes he was circumspect in his predictions), and returned home clutching a royal purse of gold. The importance of royal patronage should not be underestimated: it protected Nostradamus and popularized his prophecies. In 1559 a grand tournament was held to celebrate the marriage of the king's daughter to Philip II of Spain. Henri was wounded in a joust by Montgomery, captain of the Scottish Guard, and died of his injuries ten days later. The queen was convinced of Nostradamus's powers and when she visited Salon with her son Charles IX in 1564 she endowed Nostradamus with the title Physician in Ordinary and gave him 200 crowns.

Nostradamus died two years later, his reputation as a gifted prophet unchallenged. The definitive version of the prophecies was published by Nostradamus's pupil, Chavigny, in conjunction with the prophet's wife in 1568. Chavigny, a brilliant lawyer and theologian, went to Salon solely to study under Nostradamus in about 1554. He seems to have been close to the prophet for the rest of his life,

and it is to him that we owe the biographical details of Nostradamus's life.

Quite what prompted Nostradamus to dabble in the occult is uncertain. No-one can really be sure how he obtained his visions of the future, although he describes the practicalities of his work in the first two quatrains of the Centuries:

Sitting in secret study at night,
Alone upon the brass tripod,
A slight flame comes out of the solitude
With a promise of magic which may be
*   believed.* (I:1)

With rod in hand set in the midst of the
*   branches,*
With water he moistens both the fringe
*   and the foot.*
Fear, and a voice make me quake in my
*   sleeves:*
Divine splendor, the God is seated
*   nearby.* (I:2)

LEFT: *The second son of Henri II and Catherine de Medici, Charles IX succeeded his brother Francis II while still a minor. His mother acted as an able, if tyrannical, Regent and preserved the throne for her sons during a difficult period in French history.*

Nostradamus himself cites a mixture of divine inspiration, magic, and hereditary clairvoyance as his means of achieving visions of the future. He wrote down what he saw in four-line verses using a vocabulary that mixed French, Provençal, Latin, and Greek, in a style peppered with anagrams and classical allusions. He then arranged the quatrains in ten 'centuries' of 100 verses, apparently in random, rather than chronological, order. There are actually only 965 verses, as Century VII, with only 42 verses, is incomplete, suggesting that the prophet's work was unfinished at the time of his death. These lavish precautions not only obscured the meaning of each verse, but ensured that Nostradamus did not attract the unwarranted attentions of the Inquisition who would undoubtedly have regarded his work as diabolic. The end result, which was first published in 1568, is a fascinating collection of verses which

BELOW: *A meeting of the Grand Council of the Inquisition. The works of astrologers, prophets and soothsayers were regarded as diabolic by the Catholic Church, and the Inquisition was used to enforce the Church's displeasure.*

ABOVE: *A map of the world produced in 1570, showing the continents as Nostradamus would have imagined them.*

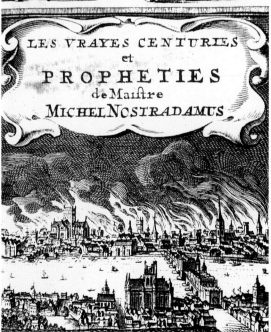

RIGHT: *The frontispiece of the first edition of the* Prophecies *to appear in England in 1668.*
The upper illustration shows the execution of Charles I in 1649, and the lower, the Great Fire of London, 1666.

apparently forecast the French Revolution, Napoleon, Hitler, and the end of the world.

Skeptics may wonder how a sixteenth-century doctor peering into a bowl of water could possibly foresee, let alone record with any degree of comprehension, something like World War II, for example. Anyone reading the less obscure quatrains will be struck immediately by the vivid visual images in them. Nostradamus lived in an age when mankind had barely got over the shock of discovering that the world was round; America was still the 'New World,' and the existence of Australia barely dreamed of; firearms were in their infancy; and the quickest mode of transport was a fast horse. Yet Nostradamus mentions air travel (I:63), a 'battle fought in the sky' (I:64), and explosions, 'distress from fire in the sky' (V:98).

Furthermore, his predictions are bound by many of the prejudices of his time. He believed that stability and peace were guaranteed by a just monarch and adherence to the Catholic Church. His

LEFT: *An eighteenth century engraving showing Catherine de Medici viewing the future in a mirror, while Nostradamus casts spells beside her.*

BELOW: *Nostradamus's son, César, reveals the fate of the Bourbons to the queen, Marie de Medici, wife of Henri IV. César never acquired the reputation of his father. Regarded by many as a charlatan, there is some doubt as to whether he inherited any of his skills.*

primary interest is the fate of France; events in other European countries, such as Britain, have to be truly extraordinary to merit a mention. The prophecies seem to deal exclusively with geographical areas within his cognizance – France and Europe, the Middle East and possibly China. Commentators do not seem to have discovered anything relating to Australia or Latin America, and references to North America are few.

Four hundred years after his death he is still famous for his extraordinary collection of prophecies that predict events from his own time until the year 3797. His contemporaries believed that he successfully foresaw the fate of the reigning Valois kings of France and, more importantly, the queen, Catherine de Medici, believed his words. Nostradamus had the confidence of the most influential person in the kingdom and the curiosity that his work provoked in sixteenth-century France has barely abated: since then the *Prophecies* have never been out of print as each generation has struggled to understand his predictions.

BRITAIN IN
THE 17TH CENTURY

ABOVE:
*Nostradamus
predicted the
upheaval of the
English Civil War.
Dario Poli's
interpretation shows
the two adversaries,
Charles I and*

*Cromwell on
opposite sides of a
raging battle, and
the other great
events in England
during the
seventeenth century,
the Plague and the
Fire of London.*

ostradamus appears to have made comparatively few predictions that concern Britain alone, but there are several verses firmly rooted in the turmoil of seventeenth-century Britain, when the political world was turned upside down by the Civil War of 1642-9. European contemporaries watched, horrified, as Charles I fought with Parliament and lost not only his throne but also his life. The *Prophecies*, incidentally, were not translated into English until 1672, and there is no record that contemporary Englishmen were aware of the century-old predictions of a French seer. Nostradamus would have taken particular interest in the English Civil War, perhaps comparing it with the turbulent religious and political events in France during his own lifetime. More importantly, the ideal for which Charles died – his belief in the divine right of kings – was something that Nostradamus upheld as one of the mainstays of a stable society.

BELOW: *One of Van Dyck's many portraits of Charles I, King of England 1625-1649.*

ABOVE: *An English coin minted during the Commonwealth, showing Cromwell's head. This is a clear indication of his position as virtual monarch after the execution of the king.*

Nostradamus had an extremely clear vision of Britain's future in the first half of the seventeenth century. He foresaw the union of Britain and Scotland under one king:

> *Le jeune né à regne Britannique,*
> *Qu'aura le père mourant recommandé,*
> *Icelui mort LONOLE donnera topique,*
> *Et à son fils le regne demandé.*

> *The young heir to the British throne,*
> *Whom his dying father will have recommended,*
> *The latter dead, LONOLE will take issue with him,*
> *And demand the realm from the son.*
> (X:40)

This quatrain is interesting for two reasons. Firstly, when Nostradamus wrote it, 'Britain' did not exist politically – England and Scotland were separate entities, and the country was not referred to as 'Britain' until the accession of James I in 1603. Secondly, as Charles Ward suggested in 1891, 'Lonole' is probably an anagram of Cromwell's nickname, 'Old Nol.' Although Cromwell did not actually lead the opposition to the king until the Civil War broke out, he was an MP for most of Charles's reign, and the relations between Charles and his parliaments were uneasy from the day he acceded to the throne in 1625 until the day he was deprived of his life by the elected representatives of his subjects. Cromwell, or 'Lonole,' did indeed demand that the king surrender control of the realm by abdicating; it was the king's refusal that led to his death.

RIGHT: *A seventeenth century etching of Charles I's execution. Nostradamus was unequivocal in his prediction in quatrain IX:49 – 'The senate of London will put their king to death.'*

Nostradamus is even more specific about the king's opponent, a man of whom he heartily disapproves:

> *Plus Macelin que roi en Angleterre,*
> *Lieu obscure né par force aura l'empire:*
> *Lâche sans foi sans loi saignera terre,*
> *Son temps s'approche si près que je soupire.*

> *More of a butcher than a king in England,*
> *From an obscure place, he will forcibly take the realm:*
> *A coward, without faith, without law, he will bleed the earth,*
> *His time approaches so near that I sigh.*
> (VIII:76)

Cromwell began life as an obscure country squire, and ended it as Lord Protector, having almost acquired the crown on his way. Nostradamus's references to butchery probably relate to the deaths caused by the Civil War, and by Cromwell's expedition to subdue Ireland in 1649.

Born in 1599, just 30 years after the death of Nostradamus, Cromwell began his political life as an influential country squire and Member of Parliament. When the crisis of the Civil War became acute, he quickly won the confidence of the army:

> *Le grand criard sans honte audacieux*
> *Sera élu gouverneur de l'armée.*
> *Le hardiesse de son contentieux*
> *Le Pont rompu, cité de peur pâmée.*

> *The great orator, boldly, without shame will be elected governor of the army.*
> *The audacity of his contention,*
> *The bridge broken, the city faint from fear.* (III:81)

Cheetham points out that there is probably one of Nostradamus's characteristic puns in this quatrain. If the words 'pont rompu' are taken back to their Latin roots, we have pons and fractus. Pontefract, in Yorkshire, was a staunchly royalist town during the Civil War, which endured two debilitating sieges by Cromwell's troops, and was in the thick of the fighting several times. Cromwell himself raised a fighting troop in his home town of Huntingdon within days of the king raising his standard at Nottingham. He gained control of the whole Parliamentary army partly through his oratory in Parliament, and partly with sheer military efficiency.

The outcome of seven years of bitter fighting is well-known. King Charles was captured in 1648, tried, found guilty of treason and executed in January the following year:

> *Gand et Bruceles marcheront contre*
> *   Anuers,*
> *Sénat de Londres mettront à mort leur*
> *   Roi.*
> *Le sel et le vin lui seront à l'envers,*
> *Pour eux avoir le regne en désarroi.*
>
> *Ghent and Brussels will march against*
> *   Antwerp,*
> *The senate of London will put their king*
> *   to death.*
> *Salt and wine will overthrow him,*
> *To have them, the realm will be turned*
> *   upside down.* (IX:49)

The number and position of this quatrain are notable. Is it mere coincidence that it is number 49, the same year as the king's execution? When Nostradamus wrote this, the English Parliament was not the powerful body it became in the 17th century – the very idea of challenging the king, let alone overthrowing him, was unthinkable. At the time of Charles's death, the Netherlands, which then included modern Belgium, were rebelling, yet again, against their Spanish masters. The salt and wine in line three refer to taxes – salt and wine being the two basic taxable commodities of the time. Charles's original dispute with Parliament did, indeed, revolve around the question of finance and taxation. There is an even clearer image of the king's fate in another verse:

> *La forteresse auprès de la Tamise*
> *Cherra par lors le Roi dedans serré.*
> *Auprès du pont sera vu en chemise*
> *Un devant mort, puis dans le fort barré*
>
> *The fortress near the Thames*
> *will fall when the king is locked inside.*
> *He will be seen near the bridge in his*
> *   shirt,*
> *One facing death, then barred inside the*
> *   fort.* (VIII:37)

After his defeat in 1648, Charles was imprisoned at Windsor Castle (on the Thames) which had fallen into the hands of the Parliamentarians. He remained there until 9 January 1649, when he was taken to London. He was executed in Whitehall on 30 January, and contemporary accounts record that he appeared on the scaffold in a thick white shirt. (Per-

ABOVE: *Charles II, 'the worthy one chased from the English realm.' Charles went into exile in 1651 and did not return to England until 1660, two years after Cromwell's death.*

haps the reference to 'the bridge' could be the platform constructed for the king's execution. The nearest bridge was London Bridge, almost two miles away). The king's supporters fled the country and Charles II went into exile to the Netherlands.

De regne Anglois le digne déchassé.
Le conseilleur par ire mis à feu.
Ses adhérants iront si bas tracer
Que le bâtard sera demi reçu.

The worthy one chased from the English
    realm.
The adviser through anger put to the fire.
His followers will stoop to such depths
That the bastard will be half-received.
    (III:80)

'The worthy one' is probably Charles II, the rightful king. After the death of Charles I royalist supporters were largely powerless to resist the all-embracing Puritan regime and in order to survive had to obey its laws. The last line is particularly interesting: shortly before his death Cromwell was actually offered (but declined) the crown. Parliament was willing to transform his position from Lord Protector to king, governing not by divine right, but by the will of Parliament and the people.

Nostradamus also foresaw two of the

most famous events in London's history, the plague of 1665 and the great fire of 1666. In an age when plague and fire were all too common, it is peculiar that he bothered to mention these occurrences. Nostradamus usually confines himself to events that are important to the whole of mankind, or affect the French nation; it seems that he regarded the deaths caused by the plague and the great fire as divine retribution for the death of an anointed king.

La grande peste de cité maritime
Ne cessera que mort ne soit vengée
Du juste sang, par prix damné sans crime
De la grand dame par feinte n'outragée.

The great plague of the maritime city
will not cease until the death is avenged
of the just blood, taken, condemned
    without crime,
of the great lady offended by deceit. (II:53)

Le sang du juste à Londres fera faute
Brûlés par foudres de vingt trois les six.
La dame antique cherra de place haute
De meme secte plusieurs seront occis.

The blood of the just will be at fault in
    London,
Burnt by lightning of three times twenty
    and six.
The old lady will fall from her high
    position,
and several of the same sect will be killed.
    (II:51)

These quatrains share some similar phrases – 'le juste sang' and, 'la dame antique/la grand dame.' The 'just blood' is Charles I; London, the maritime city devastated by fire in 1666 – 'three times twenty and six.' The Great Fire destroyed St Paul's Cathedral and caused an ancient statue of the Virgin Mary to topple from its pedestal, killing people who were sheltering from the fire.

Nostradamus produced some remarkably accurate and clear descriptions of events in Britain in the century after his death. Furthermore, the verses have a common theme running through them: that it is intrinsically wrong to remove an anointed king from his throne. Cromwell, the man who achieved this, earned divine condemnation, and retribution was exacted by sending a plague more deadly than anything seen before, and a terrible fire which engulfed a prosperous city and killed many innocent people.

FROM THE FRENCH
REVOLUTION TO NAPOLEON

BELOW:
Nostradamus devoted several quatrains to France during the Revolutionary and Napoleonic era. The Revolution (symbolized by the guillotine) was the first in a string of events which were to bathe Europe in blood. Napoleon emerged to lead France and restored French national pride.

or France the period 1789-1815 was one of turmoil, revolution and war. It was one of the most important eras in the country's history, when the upheaval of the Revolution was succeeded by the bellicose years of the Napoleonic wars. The only notable leader to emerge from the confusion was Napoleon Bonaparte, a man respected for his outstanding military skill and revered by many as the founder of modern France.

With events of this magnitude, one would expect a French prophet with any claim to credibility to provide some sort of warning of the fate that was to befall his countrymen. Nostradamus not only predicted the Revolution, but he found time to express his horror of it. For him, a conservative Catholic royalist, it was an unspeakable glimpse of a world gone mad: the king and queen beheaded, the aristocracy hounded, priests and religion outlawed. He must have wondered whether ripples in his bowl of water were clouding his vision. Napoleon also features in the quatrains (Nostradamus uses an anagram for his name in VIII:1, 'PAY, NAY, LORON...') and although Nostradamus appears to disapprove of all he stands for, he does accord him a grudging respect.

> *Regne Gaulois tu seras bien changé*
> *En lieu étrange est translaté l'empire*
> *En autres moeurs et lois seras rangé.*
> *Rouen et Chartres te seront bien du pire.*

> *Gallic realm, you will be much altered.*
> *The empire transferred to a strange place,*
> *and other customs and laws established.*
> *Rouen and Chartres will be much the*
> *worst to you.* (III:49)

In just 25 years French government was transformed and power transferred from a corrupt nobility to a Corsican soldier. Although he spent a great deal of time on the battlefield, Napoleon did not neglect home affairs. With the *Code*

Napoléon he established a new legal system based on the twin pillars of Revolutionary reform and the old Roman law. It was a middle-class system that protected property, and was a considerable change from the laws of the *ancien régime.* When Nostradamus wrote this, France was a kingdom, Napoleon established the empire he referred to.

> *De gens esclave chansons chants et*
> * requètes*
> *Captifs par Princes et Seigneurs aux*
> * prisons,*
> *À l'avenir par idiots sans têtes*
> *Seront reçus par divines oraisons.*

> *Songs, chants and requests from the*
> * enslaved people*
> *For princes and lords captured in prisons,*
> *Shall be received in the future*
> *as divine oracles by headless idiots.* (I:14)

There are certain words in this quatrain which link it very strongly to Revolutionary France: 'songs,' 'captive princes,' and 'headless.' In the early days of the Revolution the brute force of the Parisian mob governed events. The fall of the Bastille, agrarian riots and the 'bread marches' of 1789 were the first examples of the power of the common people to force change. Their actions were admired by the later Revolutionary leaders who upheld their actions with an exaggerated pride. It is worth noting that the 'Marseillaise,' the French national anthem to this day, dates from the Revolution.

> *Quand la litière du tourbillon versée*
> *Et seront faces de leurs manteaux couvers,*
> *La république par gens nouveaux vexée*
> *Lors blancs et rouges jugeront à l'envers.*

> *When the litter is overturned by the*
> * whirlwind*
> *And they will cover their faces with their*
> * cloaks,*
> *The republic will be troubled by new*
> * people*
> *Then white and red will judge in*
> * opposing ways.* (I:3)

White was the color of the royalists, red of the revolutionaries; the disunity and confused aims of the early republicans ensured that the early years of the First Republic were bloody and unstable. The first two lines of the quatrain have a double meaning. Many nobles tried to flee France, but were pulled from their carriages and litters by the mob who no doubt saw through the makeshift disguise of a cloak pulled over lavish clothes and a well-known face. The status quo was reversed: common people, driven by the whirlwind of events, quickly rose to power at the expense of the aristocracy, and, according to many commentators, hid their true aims behind a cloak of hypocrisy, corrupted by their new powers.

RIGHT: *The storming of the Bastille, 14 July 1789, is regarded as the beginning of the French Revolution. Nostradamus refers to the Revolution in several quatrains.*

ABOVE AND LEFT: *'Gallic realm you will be much changed . . .' Louis XVI refused to co-operate with the General Assembly (above) and the Christian religion was replaced by the worship of Reason: Nostradamus viewed the Revolution with mixed feelings. Shocked by the murder of the royal family, he nevertheless rejoiced in Napoleon's brief and glorious empire.*

ABOVE: *David's cartoon of the Tennis Court Oath 20 June 1789. Members of the Third Estate formed the National Assembly, vowing to draw up a constitution in the face of the king's opposition.*

RIGHT: *Queen Marie Antoinette and her children in 1787, painted by Vigée-Lebrun.*

FAR RIGHT: *The Revolutionary leader Maximilien Robespierre.*

The early revolution was not anti-monar-chical, but the king's refusal to co-operate completely with the new republican leaders inevitably led to distrust and sus-picion. Eventually, in June 1791, Louis XVI decided to flee from Paris accom-panied by his queen, Marie Antoinette, and his children. The now infamous 'Flight to Varennes' was a bungled, badly planned operation: the royal family traveled ostentatiously in a large coach with six horses – lesser mortals were re-stricted to four – and their footmen were ignorant of the geography of Paris. Nevertheless, they escaped as far as Varennes where the king was recognized; Nostradamus foretold all this in one of his most famous quatrains:

De nuit viendra par la forêt de Reines
Deux pars voltorte Herne la pierre
*   blanche.*
Le moine noir en gris dedans Varennes
Êsleu Cap. cause tempête, fue, sang,
*   tranche.*

By night will come through the forest of
*   Reines*
Two pairs, wrong route, Queen the white
*   stone.*
The monk king in gray inside Varennes
Elected Capet causes storm, fire, blood,
*   slice.* (IX:20)

There are several anagrams: Herne for reine in line two, noir for roi in line three, and Cap. short for Capetian, the kings of France from whom Louis was descended. In fact, after the Revolution the king was known as Citizen Louis Capet. Voltorte is a compound of old French volte, a route, and tort, detour. 'Foret de Reines' phonetically sounds like Varennes. The queen (where hair allegedly turned gray that night) was apparently wearing white, the ascetic king, gray, and after 1789 Louis XVI was the first French king to hold the throne by the will of a con-stitutional assembly, not just by divine right. The result of this abortive flight was terrible bloodshed, and it was the royal family who were to suffer particu-larly from the slice of the guillotine.

LEFT: *An engraving of Louis XVI, and (bottom) his execution. Found guilty of treason in December 1791, he went to the scaffold in January 1792.*

BELOW: *Marie Antoinette defends herself before the Revolutionary Council. Nostradamus called the queen's death 'an event which will outrage belief.'*

In the years immediately after the Revolution the government of France underwent several changes, and there was no clear leader until Napoleon's coup in 1799. Born in Corsica in 1769, Napoleon entered the army in 1785, and during the 1790s established a reputation as the most successful of the Republican generals. In November 1799 he forced the two parliamentary chambers to accept him as First Consul, and his autocratic rule until 1814 provided France with the first stable government in over ten years.

*Un Empereur naîtra près d'Italie
Qui à l'Empire sera vendu bien cher.
Diront avec quels gens il se rallie
Qu'on trouvera moins prince que
    bouchier.*

*An emperor will be born near Italy
who will cost the empire very dear.
The people with whom he mixes will say
he will be found less of a prince than a
    butcher.* (I:60)

This fits Napoleon very well and it is clear that Nostradamus recognizes that in this period France was an empire, rather than just a kingdom. France was almost constantly at war throughout Napoleon's reign, and generally without allies. In

terms of manpower, Napoleon's wars did France no favors – casualties were extremely high and it is to this that Nostradamus refers in the second line.

Napoleon's exploits shook France to its foundations. The country had not enjoyed international success during the eighteenth century, and Napoleon restored a sense of national pride to a country bewildered by the changes wrought by the Revolution.

> *Du nom qui onc ne fut au Roi Gaulois*
> *Jamais ne fut foudre si craintif*
> *Tremblant l'Italie, l'Espagne et les*
> *Anglois*
> *De femme étrangers grandement attentif.*
>
> *Of a name which no French king ever had*
> *Never was there so dreadful a thunderbolt*
> *Italy, Spain and the English trembling*
> *Very attractive to foreign women.* (IV:54)

During the early years of the nineteenth century Napoleon terrorized Europe, and Nostradamus, as a good Frenchman, seems quietly proud of this 'thunderbolt.' Time after time, the Germans, English, Spanish and Italians formed leagues to curb his territorial ambitions, and repeatedly they failed. The Peninsular War in Spain began to drain his resources, but it was only after the retreat from Moscow in the bitter winter of 1812 that the allies' luck began

BELOW AND BOTTOM: *The beginning of the end. Napoleon's involvement in Russia severely depleted his resources and led to his eventual defeat.*

ABOVE: *The aftermath of Austerlitz, 1805. Napoleon receives the Austrian and Russian surrender.*

to change and they eventually scored a solitary victory at Leipzig. Dynastically ambitious, Napoleon installed his siblings on several European thrones and, desperate for an heir, married first the Creole Joséphine Beauharnais in 1796, and later the Austrian Archduchess Marie-Louise.

RIGHT: *The Empress Josephine in her coronation robes. Of Creole extraction, she fulfilled Nostradamus's prediction that Napoleon would be 'attractive to foreign women.'*

*De soldat simple parviendra en empire
De robe court parviendra à la longue.
Vaillant aux armes en Église où plus
    pire,
Vexer les prêtres comme l'eau fait
    l'éponge.*

From a simple soldier he will attain the
    empire
From a short robe he will attain the long.
Valiant in arms, though much worse to
    the Church,
To annoy the priests as water does the
    sponge. (VIII:57)

Napoleon crowned himself 'Emperor of the French' in front of the Pope in December 1804. His title implied dominion over a territory greater than the old Kingdom of France and, at its zenith in 1812, Napoleon's empire stretched from Lubeck, on the Baltic, to Gaeta, south of Rome, and included a stretch of the Dalmatian coast. His bravery and success on the battlefield are undoubted; his attitude to the Church can best be described as abrasive. Although he acquired papal support for his regime, he ensured that the Catholic Church in France functioned only at the will of the state. Napoleonic bishops were forbidden to correspond with Rome without express permission of the civil power, and priests were expected to extol the virtues of the head of state and encourage loyalty to his rule from their pulpits. Such strictures were guaranteed to annoy the clergy.

Having predicted the rise of Napoleon, Nostradamus also foresaw his downfall and the result of one of the great battles of history:

> *Au mois troisième se levant le soleil*
> *Sanglier, Léopard, au champ mars pour*
>   *combattre.*
> *Léopard lassé au ciel étend son oeil*
> *Un Aigle autour du Soleil voit s'ébattre.*

> *In the third month, when the sun is rising*
> *Boar, Leopard on the field of Mars to*
>   *fight.*
> *The tired Leopard raises his eyes to the*
>   *sky*
> *where an Eagle is frolicking around the*
>   *sun.* (I:23)

The Battle of Waterloo was fought on 18 June 1815, three months after Napoleon's return to power from imprisonment on Elba. The animals refer to the heraldic devices of the combatants: the Boar is Blücher, the Prussian general; the Leopard, England; the Eagle, Napoleon. Waterloo was by no means an easy victory for the British, and by mid-afternoon when Wellington thought they were beaten, he looked up to see the

ABOVE: *A detail from David's painting of Napoleon's coronation in 1804, showing the Emperor bestowing the imperial crown on his wife, Josephine.*

LEFT: *Napoleon's most dogged adversary, the Duke of Wellington.*

French Eagles (which were carried by each regiment in the Roman style) marching forward with the body of men. This quatrain should probably be followed by I:38:

Le Sol et l'aigle au victeur paraîtront
Réponse vaine au vaincu l'on asseure
Par cor ne cris harnois n'arrêteront
Vindicte, paix par mort si achève l'heure.

The Sun and eagle will appear as victor
The vanquished is reassured with a hollow reply.
Neither horn, not shouts will stop the troops.
Vindicated, peace achieved soon through death.

Just as Napoleon's troops charged out of the sun on to the English lines, Blücher arrived with a fresh body of men, and the fighting at Waterloo continued with

ABOVE AND RIGHT:
Nostradamus devoted a whole quatrain to the Battle of Waterloo, probably because it touched on a subject dear to his heart – the defeat of France. The battle was a tough one, and only last-minute intervention by the Prussian General Blücher (above) ensured the British victory.

renewed vigor. Even when it was clear that they had lost, the French Grenadiers refused to give up or retreat. Wellington was fighting on behalf of a Europe tired of Napoleon's continual aggrandizement, and the Emperor knew he was struggling for his life. The last line implies that the high death toll of the battle was vindicated by the peace achieved through Wellington's victory, the exile of Napoleon, and his death six years later on St Helena in 1821.

NOSTRADAMUS AND
WORLD WAR II

BELOW: *Hitler and the forces of Fascism face Allied troops across the mushroom cloud of a nuclear explosion. The*

mists of war partially obscure the agonized faces of innocent victims who suffered as result of the conflict.

BELOW: *Hitler and the forces of Fascism face Allied troops across the mushroom cloud of a nuclear explosion. The mists of war partially obscure the agonized faces of innocent victims who suffered as result of the conflict.*

he appearance of Adolf Hitler in the prophecies is one of the things that has ensured continued interest in Nostradamus during the past 50 years. It is by no means unusual for famous men to believe that their actions or 'greatness' were pre-destined, but Hitler is probably the most notorious of this select group and, unlike others, he appears to have been correct in his presumption. In verse II:24 Nostradamus uses the word 'Hister,' something that has been seized upon by supporters of Nostradamus as proof positive of his ability. Scholars of the prophecies have remarked that Nostradamus frequently used anagrams of words, occasionally adding one bogus letter, hence 'Hister' for Hitler. However, it is worth mentioning that this word was also used by the Romans in reference to the Lower Danube. In this context, however, a river seems nonsensical, and it seems more likely that 'Hister' is an anagram for Hitler.

Bêtes farouches de faim fleuves tranner,
Plus part du champ encontre Hister sera.
En cage de fer le grand fera traîner
Quand rien enfant de Germain observera.

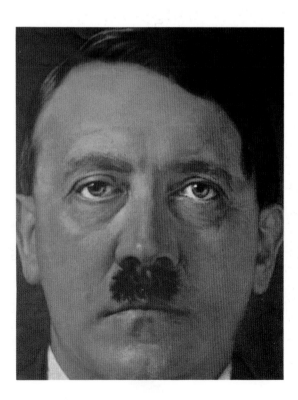

LEFT: *Adolf Hitler, referred to by Nostradamus as 'Hister'.*

Low Countries in an effort to boost the morale of the beleaguered populace.

Translatera en la Grande Germanie
Brabant et Flandres, Gand, Bruges, et
*   Boulogne.*
La trêve feinte, le grand Duc d'Armenie
Assaillira Vienne et la Cologne.

He will transfer into greater Germany
Brabant and Flanders, Ghent, Bruges,
*   and Boulogne.*
The truce, a sham, the great duke of
*   Armenia*
will attack Vienna and Cologne. (V:94)

Hitler's ambition (and his excuse for invading Austria, Czechoslovakia and Poland) was to incorporate areas of neighboring countries with German-speaking populations into 'Gross Deutschland' – which sounds uncannily like 'Greater Germany.' In May 1940 Hitler transferred his attention from Poland to the west – France, the Low Countries and Britain. The 'duke of Armenia' probably refers to Russia, which was allied with the Germans until June 1941 when Hitler launched Operation Barbarossa against his former ally. At the end of the war, when the Soviet Union was part of the Allied force, Russian troops invaded Germany from the East, meeting their American allies in the southeast.

ABOVE: *Magda Goebbels with two of her children. The wife of Hitler's propaganda chief, Joseph Goebbels, it was Magda who first discovered the references to Hitler in the Prophecies.*

ABOVE RIGHT AND OPPOSITE: *Germany rearmed heavily during the 1930s and accompanied this with excellent propaganda.*

Beasts wild with hunger will cross rivers.
The greater part of the field will be against Hitler.
The great one will be dragged in an iron cage
when the child of Germany observes nothing. (II:24)

'Wild beasts' is a reference to German troops, who swarmed over a Europe largely united against Hitler. The last line is interesting if one remembers that the majority of Germans claim that they knew nothing of the worst aspects of Hitler's regime.

Hitler was introduced to the prophecies by Joseph Goebbels, his Minister of Propaganda, and the Nazis used the predictions for their own sinister ends as early as 1936. During the Blitzkrieg of 1940, when it was clear that quatrain V:94 was all too true, the Allies produced fake prophecies which they dropped on the

The next quatrain is, admittedly, less precise than many and could be applied to several other people. However, Hitler was born to a poor family in Austria and obtained a following in the confusion of postwar Germany because of his mesmeric speeches and tirades against the Jews and the Treaty of Versailles.

Du plus profond de l'occident d'Europe
De pauvres gens un jeune enfant naîtra
Qui par sa langue séduira grande troupe.
Son bruit au regne d'Orient plus croîtra.

In the depths of Western Europe,
a young child will be born of poor people,
who will seduce many people with his
oratory.
His reptuation will grow even greater in
the kingdom of the East. (III:35)

BELOW: *Hitler addressing the 1934 Nuremberg rally. A mesmeric public speaker, Hitler was expert at raising the atmosphere at Nazi rallies to fever pitch.*

Cheetham believes that the last line is confirmation that this quatrain refers to Hitler. Hitler was respected in the East – Japan allied with Germany, and was sympathetic to her from the mid-1930s.

A French commentator of the 1930s, Max de Fontbrune, found a great deal about Hitler and the Nazis in the *Prophecies*, so much, indeed, that his book was banned in 1940 by the Vichy government as M. de Fontbrune's commentary was less than complimentary about the Fascist powers around him. Like Nostradamus himself, he was concerned primarily with France and contemporary events, so he attributed a large number of prophecies to the troubled times of the 1930s and 1940s. This is one of them:

Près du grand fleuve grand fosse, terre
egeste,
En quinze pars sera l'eau divisée:
La cité prise, feu, sang, crise conflit
mettre,
Et la plupart concerne au collisee.

Near the great river, a great ditch, earth
dug up.
The water will be divided into 15 parts:
the city taken, fire, blood, cries, battle
given,
and the greater part concerned with
collision. (IV:80)

This quatrain is another vivid one, and refers to the Maginot Line, the defenses built by the French in the interwar period to protect against another German invasion. The fortifications lay along the eastern frontier of France, but did not connect with the Belgian border because the Ardennes were thought to provide a sufficiently strong natural defense. When the Germans invaded in 1940 they by-passed the Maginot Line, invaded Belgium and northern France through the Ardennes, and within a month had seized Paris.

By June 1940 most of Europe was under Hitler's control and Britain stood alone against the might of the Third Reich. Nostradamus foresaw this isolation:

*Ceux dans les îles de longtemps assiégés
Prendront vigueur force contre ennemis.
Ceux par dehors mort de faim profligés
En plus grande faim que jamais seront
    mis.*

*Those besieged in the islands for a long
    time
will act forcefully against their enemies.
Those outside will die of hunger,
    overcome
by such starvation as never before known.*
  (III:71)

Although Hitler did not attempt to invade Britain after 1940, the German
U-boats did their utmost to restrict the
movement of Allied shipping. Crossing
the Atlantic was perilous, as was the
voyage south to the Mediterranean.
Britain did, however, succeed in acting
'forcefully against her enemies,' and kept

ABOVE: *Hitler's
regime promised
jobs and prosperity
to a Germany worn
down by war
reparations, which
partly explains his
wide appeal.*

LEFT: *German
troops in Paris,
1940. The speed
with which the
forces of the
Wehrmacht invaded
France and the Low
Countries
astonished onlookers
throughout Europe.*

THIS PAGE: *'Those besieged in the islands for a long time will act forcefully against their enemies'. After the Fall of France in 1940, Britain was effectively the only European power still able to fight Germany. German U-boats patrolled the Atlantic (above right and right), doing their best to prevent American food and supplies reaching Britain. The cartoon above shows a defiant Winston Churchill determined to hold out against the Nazi menace.*

LEFT: *The ruins of Hiroshima after the explosion of the first atomic bomb. Nostradamus foresaw 'Living fire . . . inside globes', but even he could not have imagined the dreadful destruction and suffering caused by nuclear weapons.*

BELOW: *Inmates of Dachau concentration camp, 1938. The Nazis imprisoned Jews and political opponents before World War II, but saved the real atrocities for wartime.*

the sea lanes open. Indeed, Britain was comparatively well-off compared to those in occupied Europe where, by 1945, food was universally scarce. The last two lines may refer to the Nazi concentration camps where many of those who were not gassed simply starved to death.

World War II was the most terrible conflict mankind has ever known. Fifty years later we are still horrified by the sheer number of dead and the extent of the destruction. Imagine, then, how this war must have appeared to a man of the sixteenth century:

Sera laissé feu vif, mort caché,
Dedans les globes horrible épouvantable.
De nuit à classe cité en poudre lache
La cité à feu, l'ennemi favorable.

Living fire will be unleashed, hidden death,
frightful, horrible, inside globes.
By night the city will be reduced to dust by the fleet
The city in flames, the enemy amenable.
    (V:8)

A bomber's eye view. Vapor trails (right) were a common sight over the skies of Europe and Britain in 1940. Nostradamus anticipated the invention of airplanes and wrote of a 'battle fought in the skies,' remarkable predictions for a man of the sixteenth century.

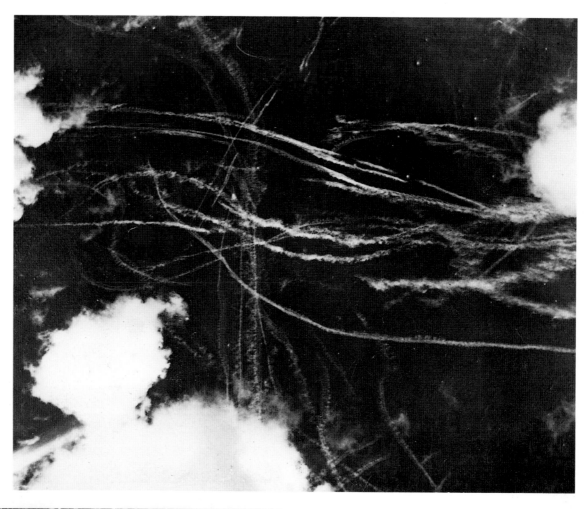

This quatrain conveys the terror and confusion that must be felt by anyone under fire. 'Living fire inside globes' is one of the most apt descriptions of bombs, and one only has to look at photographs of cities like Coventry, Dresden or Hiroshima in 1945 to see that the rubble remaining is little more than the dust of the original buildings. Nostradamus also described aerial battles, perhaps envisaging the blazing debris of a plane shot out of the sky:

De nuit soleil penseront avoir vu
Quand le pourceau demi-homme on verra.
Bruit, chant, bataille, au ciel battre
*   aperçu,*
Et bêtes brutes à parler l'on orra.

At night they will think they have seen
*   the sun*
when they see the pig half-man.
Noise, song, battle, fighting seen in the
*   sky,*
and one will hear brute beasts talking.
*   (I:64)*

An oxygen mask (particularly one from the 1940s) is not unlike a snout and gives the wearer a porcine look. The 'brute beasts talking' probably refers to radio communication between the airplanes. Nostradamus may have found this whole glimpse incredibly confusing, but his description provides a naïve and graphic picture of a dogfight.

The prophet's perceptions of bombing and aerial battles are astounding enough, but it is the accuracy of Hitler's name that strikes most readers of Nostradamus's prophecies as one of the most remarkable aspects of his work.

ABOVE: *Nagasaki under atomic-bomb attack, 9 August 1945.*

ABOVE LEFT AND LEFT: *The aftermath of war in the Far East was horrific. General Douglas MacArthur (above left) surveys the damage in Manila, but this was negligible in comparison with that in Hiroshima (left) and Nagasaki.*

THE END OF THE
20TH CENTURY

BELOW: *Nostradamus hinted that the volatile Middle East would be crucial to the political balance of power. The shifting sands of the desert mimic the uneasy political situation and the influence of the USA, represented by the Statue of Liberty, hovers over the region.*

any commentators believe that Nostradamus had a special interest in events at the end of the twentieth century because of the proximity of the millennium. Apart from anything else, this century has seen astounding technological advances that have completely altered the way we live. Nostradamus not only foresaw these immense changes, but also succeeds in describing them, despite the fact that what he saw in the murky waters of his divining bowl must have been both frightening and puzzling.

> *Les fléaux passés diminue le monde.*
> *Longtemps la paix terres inhabitées.*
> *Sur marchera par ciel, terre, mer et onde,*
> *Puis de nouveau les guerres suscitées.*

> With pestilence passed, the world becomes
>   smaller.
> For a long time peace over inhabited
>   lands,
> One will cross through the skies, over
>   land, sea and waves,
> Then wars will start up once more. (I:63)

This is a fairly good description of the postwar world. Despite a profusion of

BELOW: *The United Nations in action. Since its formation in 1945, the UN has striven to preserve world peace by mediating in areas of political tension. The UN has done much to fulfil Nostradamus's prophecy that peace will reign over 'inhabited lands.'*

small conflicts, there has not been a truly major war during the last 50 years, and mass tourism has meant that people can travel great distances safely and quickly. The sheer size of the earth is now a minimal problem in communications; inventions like the jet engine and the satellite mean that America is only a matter of hours from Europe, or a split-second connection on the phone line. It may be that this comparatively halcyon period is coming to an end: unrest in eastern Europe and the Gulf are conflicts that the major powers cannot ignore.

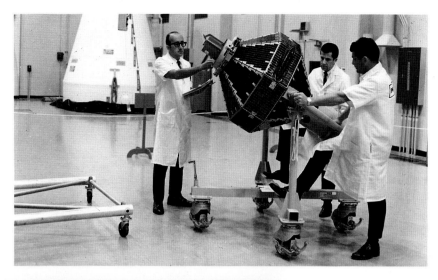

ABOVE AND LEFT: *Communications satellites are inventions beyond even Nostradamus's remarkable powers of perception. He did, however, realize how important machines would be to twentieth-century living when he mentioned a creature that 'lives without having any feeling.'*

FAR LEFT: *'One will cross through the skies . . .' Air travel has become so common that the skies of Northern Europe are now dangerously busy. It is now possible to travel great distances in a matter of hours, particularly in supersonic planes like Concorde (below left), journeys that would have taken Nostradamus and his contemporaries months.*

ABOVE AND RIGHT: *The eruption of the American volcano Mount St Helens in 1980. Debris could be seen as far away as New York (right) as the prophet predicted in quatrain I:87. There are several unfulfilled prophecies that may relate to the USA and New York in particular, none of them very pleasant. Quatrain X:49 promises poison in the water system and IX:92 a siege.*

People of the middle ages and the Renaissance believed that natural phenomena like comets or earthquakes were signs of divine displeasure or, occasionally, approval. Nostradamus naturally applied this orthodoxy to his predictions:

Ennosigée feu du centre de terre
Fera trembler autour de cité neuve.
Deux grands rochers longtemps feront la
  guerre
Puis Arethuse rougira nouveau fleuve.

Earthquaking fire from the center of the
  earth
Will make the new city tremble.
Two great rocks will war for a long time,
then Arethusa will redden the river once
  more. (I:87)

This quatrain needs brief explanation: 'Ennosigée' comes from the Latin '*Ennosigaeus*,' the 'earthshaker.' Cheetham believes that this quatrain refers to the eruption of Mount St Helens in 1980, and that the 'new city' is New York. Despite the great distance between the volcano and New York, volcanic dust and ash polluted the 'new city.' At the time of the eruption, not only were relations between the United States and the Soviet Union poor (and had been so for years), but the war between Iran and Iraq had just begun, and two more immovable and rock-like combatants it would be hard to find, given the long stalemate that existed during the 1980s. Their dispute over the Shatt al'Arab meant that the blood of thousands of men was spilled in the delta of the Tigris and Euphrates. So it seems that Nostradamus regarded the Mount St Helens eruption as a harbinger of war in the Middle East.

Although Nostradamus does not appear to make many specific predictions for America, he has not ignored the immense influence of the world's richest country. He devotes several quatrains to the balance of power between the United States and the Soviet Union, and to the demise of the Cold War. Ten years ago the quatrains relating to the decline of Communism and the alliance between American and Russian statesmen seemed completely unbelievable but, once again, his predictions appear to be uncannily accurate:

*L'oiseau royal sur la cité solaire
Sept mois devant fera nocturne augure.
Mur d'orient cherra tonnerre éclair,
Sept jours aux portes les ennemis à
    l'heure.*

*The royal bird over the city of the sun
will deliver a nocturnal omen seven
    months before.
The wall in the East will fall – thunder
    and lightning.
In seven days the enemies [will be]
    directly at the gates.* (V:81)

This is clearly about the fall of the Berlin Wall in November 1989, and the subsequent decline of the Communist regimes in eastern Europe. Berlin, as the former capital of imperial Germany, was littered with Prussian eagles on buildings and monuments, symbols of the power of the Kaiser (and later the Nazis). As soon as the wall was down, the East German people (former enemies of the West), unable to believe their luck, flooded into West Berlin intent on at least seeing the wealth of the West, if not actually emigrating. The generosity of the West German government towards the impoverished East Germans has led to a feeling of resentment among West Germans, who feel that their hard-earned

wealth is going to support a weak economy that is little more than a money-pit. Officially the Germans are now united, but there is still a feeling of antipathy between East and West, hence Nostradamus's reference to 'the enemies at the gate.'

The fall of the Berlin Wall was only one part of the improvement in relations between Western powers and those behind the Iron Curtain. With Mikhail Gorbachev's rise to power, the Soviet Union and the USA decelerated the arms race, and diplomatic ties between the two Superpowers are now closer than they have been in any other period.

*Un jour seront demis [d'amis] les deux
    grands maîtres,
Leur grand pouvoir se verra augmenté:
La terre neuve sera en ses hauts êtres,
Au sanguinaire le nombre raconté.*

*One day the two great masters will be
    friends,
Their great power will be seen to
    increase:
The new world will be at the height of its
    power,
To the man of blood the numbers are
    recounted.* (II:89)

RIGHT AND BELOW:
The initial euphoria after the fall of the Berlin Wall in 1989 was succeeded by new problems for Germany. In addition to an influx of East Germans into the West German workforce, the cost of maintaining the weak East German economy is a heavy burden on West Germany.

As a rough summary of the state of the world in the early 1990s, this is far from inaccurate. If not actually allied, the United States and the Soviet Union (or Russian Federation) have given similar reactions to events like the Gulf War or the Yugoslavian civil war. The peaceful and constructive influence of the United States over the world has rarely been stronger. The identity of 'the man of blood' is unclear; Gorbachev is a likely candidate. His birthmark on his forehead really does make him seem like a marked man, one fated to do something remarkable. His achievements were considerable, but since his resignation at the end of 1991 it seems unlikely that he will continue to be of great importance.

Gorbachev's reforms paved the way for the most monumental upheaval in Russian history since 1917: the dissolution of the Soviet Union at the end of 1991.

Le regne à deux laissé bien peu tiendront,
Trois ans sept mois passés feront la
*   guerre.*
Les deux Vestales contre rebelleront,
Victor puis né en Armonique terre.

*The rule left to two, they will hold it for
  a short time.
After three years and seven months they
  will go to war.
The two vassals will rebel against them.
The victor born in the land of Armenia.*
  (IV:95)

The federation formed in December 1991 by the former states of the Soviet Union enjoys an uneasy unity, and at the time of writing is dominated by Russia and the Ukraine, the largest and wealthiest republics. One of the most compelling problems is the federation's struggle to reach agreement over the control of nuclear weapons positioned throughout the former Soviet Union. A serious disagreement over such a basic matter of defense has serious implications for the whole world. There is already trouble in the smaller republics, which are loath to submit to Russian overlordship. The last line seems to preclude Boris Yeltsin from lasting success; Edvard Shevardnaze, who comes from neighboring Georgia, is the only statesman who was born anywhere near Armenia.

ABOVE AND LEFT:
The rise of younger, more pragmatic politicians in the Kremlin during the mid-1980s opened up a new era in East-West relations. Mikhail Gorbachev and Ronald Reagan made substantial arms reductions, while the Soviet Foreign Minister Edvard Shevardnadze (above) helped to convince the West that the Soviet Union was no longer an 'evil empire.'

ABOVE AND RIGHT: *Nostradamus succinctly summed up Saddam Hussein in quatrain VIII:70: 'He will enter, wicked, infamous villain, tyrannizing over Mesopotamia …' Saddam failed to realize that he had provoked the Western powers once too often and was possibly surprised by the reaction to his invasion of Kuwait in August 1990.*

Nostradamus's predictions for the late twentieth century recognize that the world will effectively be governed by two powers or ideologies, but that smaller countries will still be able to challenge this rule. It is often these lesser powers who cause the most trouble, as was evident in August 1990, when Saddam Hussein of Iraq invaded Kuwait. Nostradamus predicted not only the resulting war, but the build-up to it as well.

*Le prince Arabe Mars, Sol, Venus,
   Lion,
Regne d'Eglise par mer succombera.
Devers la Perse bien près d'un million,
Bisance, Egypte ver.serp, invadera.*

The Arab prince Mars, the sun, Venus,
   Leo,
The rule of the church will succumb by
   sea.
Very nearly a million men towards
   Persia,
The true serpent will invade Byzantium
   and Egypt. (V:25)

Saddam Hussein of Iraq easily qualifies for the title of 'The Arab prince of Mars': Iraq has been at war throughout most of his years in power and he has done everything possible to acquire the most up-to-date military hardware available, failing only in his attempts to procure nuclear capability. With conscription for every young man, the size of the Iraqi army was huge, and Saddam himself boasted that it was one-million strong. In July 1990 he positioned large numbers of troops on the Kuwaiti border to intimidate the Kuwaitis into decreasing their oil production, and invaded the small Gulf state (which borders Iran and Saudi Arabia, as well as Iraq) on 2 August 1990 (when the sun was in Leo). Universally condemned, the Iraqi troops awaited the onslaught of the Western powers, which began in January 1991.

*Il entrera vilain, méchant, infame,
Tyrannisant la Mesopotamie
Tous amis fait d'adulterine dame,
Terre horrible noir de physionomie.*

He will enter, wicked, infamous villain,
Tyrannizing over Mesopotamia.
All friends made by the adulterous
woman.
The land horrible and black in
appearance. (VIII:70)

Nostradamus has here summed up the
Gulf conflict quite succinctly. Saddam
Hussein has ruled Iraq – which covers the
area of ancient Mesopotamia – corruptly
and viciously for many years. When it
was clear that he was going to lose the

battle for Kuwait to the Allies, he ordered that the oil wells in the region be ignited. This caused untold environmental damage, and literally turned the land and the sky black with noxious smoke from the burning oil.

ABOVE, LEFT AND FAR LEFT: *Casualties of the Gulf War are numbered in their thousands, but not all were human. Saddam's orders to ignite the Kuwaiti oil wells polluted a large area of the northern Persian Gulf with both oil slicks and dense, black fumes, and killed marine and bird life.*

Unfortunately the struggle in the Middle East is still far from finished. Nostradamus not only hinted that the third world war would have its roots in this region, but also that the Antichrist would emerge from this area.

APOCALYPSE – NOW?

BELOW:
Nostradamus predicts a dreadful fate for mankind at the end of the twentieth century. A red hot sun burns

down on a landscape ruined by war and environmental disaster. The giant hand symbolizes humanity's struggle for survival.

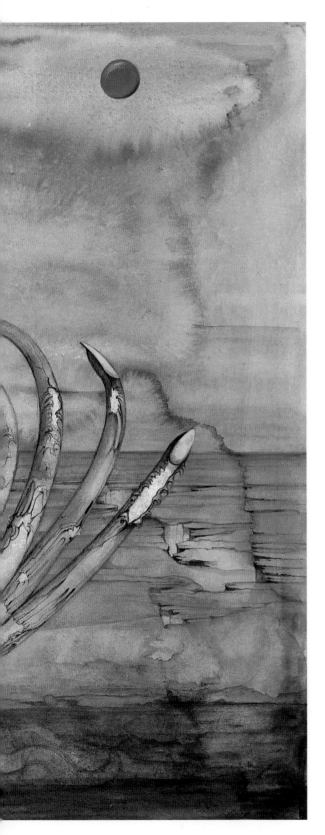

o a man of the sixteenth century there was something almost mystical about the millennium. Immediately before the year 1000 AD, peasants apparently abandoned their work, and many people sat back to await the end of the world which the Church had told them was imminent. It is partly for this reason that so many of Nostradamus's quatrains imply that the end, for those of us living in the 1990s, is definitely nigh. What is slightly uncanny is his general belief that a war centering on Middle Eastern problems will provoke the apocalypse. During the sixteenth century, Christian Europeans acknowledged the military threat from the Moors and Ottoman Turks who hovered menacingly on Europe's borders, so this is not a new idea. Nostradamus's predictions for the end of this century, however, seem disturbingly precise.

Concurrent with the threat from the Arab world is a decline in both the fortunes and morals of the Vatican. Nostradamus, following the tradition of the eleventh century Irish prophet Malachy, believed that there will be only two more popes after the present incumbent. He paints a

BELOW:
Nostradamus's prophecies relating to the Apocalypse were inevitably influenced by the beliefs of his time. This etching shows a sixteenth-century astronomer at work, with a comet soaring across the sky behind him.

BELOW: *Pope John-Paul I died after only a month in office in 1978. The circumstances surrounding his death are still puzzling and Nostradamus hinted at foul play in quatrain III:65.*

dark picture of papal politics and seems to have predicted the death of John-Paul I (murdered? III:65, IV:11) and the assassination attempts on John-Paul II, V:49, X:65. He links the fall of the papacy to the rise of the Antichrist and the terrible events that will occur around the year 2000.

He seems convinced that mankind will be in terrible trouble at the end of this century:

Faux à l'étang joint vers le Sagittaire
En son haut AUGE de l'exaltation.
Peste, famine, mort de main militaire.
Le siècle approche de rénovation.

A scythe joined with a pond in Sagittarius
at the high point of its ascendancy.
Plague, famine, death from the military arm.
The century approaches its renewal. (I:16)

FAR LEFT: *Van Eyck's* Last Judgment *shows the orthodox view of heaven and hell in Nostradamus's time.*

LEFT: *Pope John-Paul II blesses a crowd in his native Poland. The first non-Italian pope for several centuries, John-Paul II has not enjoyed an entirely easy pontificate. Nostradamus predicted the assassination attempt of 1981 and hints in X:65 that the papacy's 'ruin approaches.'*

This quatrain provides an exact astrological reference: the first line refers to the conjunction of Saturn with Aquarius in Sagittarius towards the end of the century. The word 'renewal' suggests the millennium. To Roberts, writing from the safe distance of 1947, this implied 1999. This is a theme that Nostradamus returns to several times over. Grim times apparently lie ahead, and events will take a turn for the worse when we least expect it:

Après grand trouble humain, plus grand
    s'apprête
Le grand moteur les siècles renouvèle;
Pluie, sang, lait, famine, fer et peste,
Au ciel vu feu courant longue étincelle.

After great trouble for mankind, worse
    approaches
As the great mover renews the centuries;
Rain, blood, milk, famine, steel and
    plague,
Fire is seen running through the sky with
    long sparks. (II:46)

Having survived unspecified problems, a comet will appear to warn mankind of the war to come. Nostradamus is blunt about events around the turn of the century: 'rain, blood, milk, famine, steel and plague' – in other words, disaster.

The reason for this depressing outlook is simple – mankind can expect the arrival of the Antichrist to drive them toward death and destruction. Nostradamus often refers to a dark man from the east, and pinpoints the beginning of his reign:

L'an mil neuf cent nonante neuf sept mois
Du ciel viendra un grand roi d'effrayeur
Ressusciter le grand roi d'Angolmois,
Avant après Mars regner par bonheur.

In the seventh month of the year 1999,
A great king of terror will come from the
    sky
To revitalize the great king of the
    Mongols,
Before and after Mars reigns with success.
    (X:72)

ABOVE: *It seems impossible that the wealthy western world will be destroyed by famine, but man-made weapons may yet achieve this. Nostradamus seems convinced that the last years of this century will be truly terrible for all mankind.*

FAR LEFT: *Nostradamus mentions famine many times. Population appears to have outstripped resources in many areas of Africa, and famine has become an annual occurrence.*

This is one of the most unequivocal statements in the whole of the *Prophecies*, but of course, only time will tell whether or not it is accurate. This is one of the few quatrains with a precise date, a year that de Fontbrune suggests is the end of the Christian era. Several commentators have suggested that 'Angolmois' is an anagram for the French word, Mongolois – Mongols. So the king of terror, or anti-christ will be a figure reminiscent of Genghis Khan, the greatest king the Mongols ever had, and not a man known for his pacific nature. However, his appearance will not herald an immediate end to the world – war will continue after the Antichrist's arrival.

Libra verra regner Hesperies
De ciel et terre tenir la monarchie.
D'Asie forces nul ne verra péries
Que sept ne tiennent par rang la
 hiérarchie.

Libra will be seen to rule the West
And to hold the monarchy of the heavens
 and earth.
No one will see the forces of Asia perish
Until seven hold the hierarchy in order.
(IV:50)

ABOVE AND RIGHT:
Nostradamus has predicted that the Antichrist will emerge from the East. An alliance between the Chinese and the nations of Islam may seem unlikely, but they do share an intense distrust of America and the Western powers.

This quatrain may explain the forebearance of the West when threatened by an increasingly powerful military force of the East. Libra, the balance, representing good sense, will prevent the West from striking out until an unspecified regime has undergone seven changes of leadership. However, this attitude will soon erode, as the Antichrist pushes mankind to the edge of the abyss:

Sur les rochers sang on verra pleuvoir
Sol Orient, Saturne Occidental.
Près d'Orgon guerre, à Rome grand mal
*   voir,*
Nefs parfondrées, et pris le Tridental.

One will see blood rain on the rocks,
Sun in the East, Saturn in the West.
War near Orgon, great evil to be seen in
*   Rome,*
Ships sunk, the trident taken. (V:62)

The Antichrist will embroil the world in a war more terrible than anything that has gone before, and destroy the papacy, too. In another quatrain, Nostradamus implies that New York will burn: 'The sky will burn at 45 degrees/ Fire approaches the New City' (VI:97); as we

ABOVE: *The President of the USA is never far away from the closely-guarded briefcase containing the codes necessary to launch a nuclear strike, and inevitably, the third world war.*

LEFT: *A Polaris nuclear submarine launches a missile. Nostradamus mentions 'weapons and letters concealed in a fish' – a description which could relate to a submarine.*

have seen from predictions made in earlier quatrains, mankind will totter on the brink of extinction, but there is considerable hope that the forces of evil will be defeated:

> *Mars et le sceptre se trouvera conjoint*
> *Dessous Cancer calamiteuse guerre.*
> *Un peu après sera nouveau Roi oint*
> *Qui par longtemps pacifiera la terre.*

> *Mars and the scepter will be found united*
> *Under Cancer a calamitous war.*
> *A short time later a new king will be*
>   *anointed*
> *Who will pacify the earth for a long time.*
>   (VI:24)

The scepter stands for Jupiter, and the next conjunction with Mars occurs (according to Wollner) on 21 June 2002. Quatrain X:72 mentions calamity in the summer and contains a rare promise of peace after a war, which does signify that life continues after the millennium.

LEFT, FAR LEFT AND ABOVE: *Weapons of mass destruction like the Titan missile (far left) were constructed in their thousands during the years of the Cold War, culminating in the USA's 'Star Wars' program (above and left), Since the rapprochement between the former Soviet Union and the USA in the mid-1980s, many of these armaments have been destroyed.*

POST-APOCALYPSE

BELOW: *Nostradamus indicates that mankind will survive the devastation of the late twentieth century, but in a* *greatly reduced state. Humanity will still regard technology, symbolized by the rocket, as the solution to its problems.*

Nostradamus has predicted dire things for mankind at the end of this century. But many of his predictions seem to extend beyond the arrival of the Antichrist in 1999, so it seems probable that mankind survives his onslaught:

Vingt ans du regne de la Lune passés,
Sept mil ans autre tiendra sa monarchie.
Quand le soleil prendra ses jours lassés
Lors accomplit et mine ma prophétie.

Twenty years of the reign of the moon
* have passed*
and another will take up his rule for 7000
* years.*
When the sun takes up its exhausted days,
then my prophecies will end and be
* accomplished.* (I:48)

Commentators disagree about how to date this particular prophecy, but it is interesting that, like modern astronomers, Nostradamus thought that the sun will eventually burn itself out.

He foresees environmental problems, war, and a new religious leader. Europe will suffer an influx of refugees, possibly because of famine elsewhere.

BELOW: *The sun sets over a tank in the Arabian desert, symbols of the two greatest threats to the well-being of mankind: warfare and global warming.*

ABOVE AND RIGHT:
*The trials of life
and death in a
Kurdish refugee
camp, 1991.
Millions of dollars
of Western aid still
cannot provide a
homeland for this
dispossessed people.
If Nostradamus's
predictions
concerning the post-
Apocalyptic world
are correct, this
problem will be
magnified many
times.*

*Tours, Orléans, Blois, Angers, Reims et
   Nantes
Cités vexées par subit changement:
Par langues étranges seront tendues tentes,
Fleuves, dards, Rennes, terre et mer
   tremblement.*

*Tours, Orléans, Blois, Angers, Reims
   and Nantes
will be cities troubled by a sudden change:
Tents will be pitched by those of a foreign
   tongue,
Rivers, darts at Rennes, the earth and the
   sea quake.* (I:20)

The invasion of Europe by refugees from the second or third world is not a particularly outrageous idea. Asia and Africa suffer annual floods and famines; the beleaguered citizens of Soviet Republics are short of food, and the Kurds, hounded by Saddam Hussein and driven from their homes by war, have already descended upon Turkey. Given the affluence of the West, it is hardly surprising that the hungry and deprived of the world look upon the USA and Europe with envious eyes.

Unfortunately, Nostradamus also predicts worldwide starvation. In the late twentieth century, scientists have issued myriad warnings about the pollution of the environment. Global warming, deforestation, and the poisoning of the food chain are terms with which we are all familiar, but the problems themselves are apparently not yet severe enough for us to treat them seriously. Our neglect may prove fatal for our grandchildren:

*La grande famine que je sens approcher,
Souvent tourner, puis être universelle,
Si grande et longue qu'on viendra arracher
Du bois racine et l'enfant de mamelle.*

*The great famine that I sense
   approaching,
Often turning, then becoming universal,
will be on such a large scale and last so
   long
that one will pull roots from the woods,
   and children from the breast.* (I:67)

Whether this disaster will be caused by environmental problems or because of a breakdown of society as a result of war is uncertain.

Nostradamus appears to have foreseen the dominance of computer technology on our lives, and realized the dangers inherent in our reliance on machines. The world's nuclear power – both weapons and generators – is controlled by microchips, and it is not beyond reasonable doubt that a fault in the system could prove fatal for a great many people.

Ce qui vivra et n'ayant aucun sens
Viendra léser à mort son artifice.
Autun, Châlon, Langres et les deux Sens
La grêle et glace fera grand maléfice.

That which will live without having any
*   feeling,*
Will be killed through its own artifice.
At Autun, Châlon, Langres and the two
*   Sens*
Hail and ice will cause a great deal of
*   damage. (I:22)*

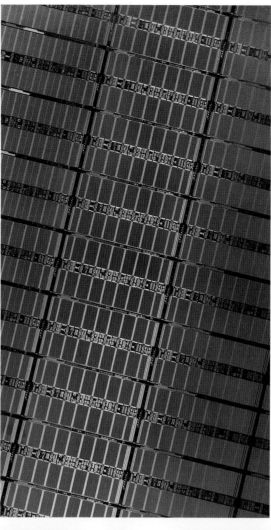

LEFT AND BELOW: *Powerful microchips (left) control many areas of our lives including nuclear power plants (below) and weapons. In quatrain I:22 Nostradamus envisages the failure of a powerful machine and the terrible consequences which will ensue.*

Something that lives 'without feeling' is an ingenious interpretation of a vision that must have puzzled the seer. 'Hail and ice' could represent radioactive dust present in the air after an explosion at a nuclear-power station.

Nostradamus foresees explosions in and around France which will devastate large areas, and he produces haunting images of fish boiling in the rivers.

A quarante-huit degré climatérique,
À fin de Cancer si grande sécheresse;
Poisson en mer, fleuve, lac cuit hectique
Bearn, Bigorre, par feu ciel en détresse.

At the 48th climacteric degree,
at the end of Cancer there is such great dryness;
Fish in the sea, rivers and lakes boil hectically
Béarn, Bigorre distressed by fire from the sky. (V:98)

It is worth noting that Béarn and Bigorre were counties in southwest France which belonged to the House of Bourbon. 'The heat of the sun' mentioned in II:3 may be more intense in these areas simply because of global warming. If the ozone layer continues to shrink at its current rate, the south of France will have

LEFT AND BELOW: *Many cities suffer terrible pollution, as at Denver (below), and ozone levels can be monitored with special photographic methods (far left). Black and red represent low ozone values.*

BELOW FAR LEFT: *Silicon Valley, California, home of the computer chip.*

a climate akin to that of the Sahara desert by the end of the 21st century: a drought around the 48th parallel (which runs through northern France) would not, therefore, be unlikely. However, 'distress from fire in the sky' seems to be a clear reference to a nuclear explosion over south-western France, and it may be this that is responsible for the starvation in the Mediterranean mentioned in the next quatrain.

Pour la chaleur solaire sur la mer,
De Negrepont les poissons demi cuits.
Les habitants les viendront entamer
Quant Rhod. et Gennes leur faudra le biscuit.

Because of the heat of the sun on the sea the fishes around Negrepont will be half-cooked.
The local people will eat them when food fails in Rhodes and Genoa.
(II:3)

Negrepont was the Venetian name for their colony in Greece. Famine and plague, probably as a result of nuclear war, will also cripple Greece:

Dans les Cyclades, en Perinthe et Larisse,
Dedans Sparte tout le Péloponnesse,
Si grande famine, peste par faux connisse,
Neuf mois tiendra et tout le chersonèse.

In the Cyclades, in Perinthus and Larissa in Sparta and the whole Peloponnese,
Such a great famine and plague through false dust,
will last nine months throughout the whole peninsula. (V:90)

Athens is already suffering from another sort of 'false dust' – smog. Cars are regularly banned from the city center because the build-up of fumes is too dangerous. Life in the Mediterranean seems set to become even more bleak,

ABOVE:
Czechoslovakian children wear face masks to protect them against the poor quality of the air.

RIGHT AND FAR RIGHT: *The rain forests of South America are being cut down at an alarming rate, destroying not only vital flora and fauna, but also the traditions of ancient tribes. Encouraged by environmentalists, local people try to fight back (far right).*

with Nostradamus painting even gloomier pictures of a post-holocaust landscape:

Depuis Monech jusqu'auprès de Sicille
Toute la plage demeurra désolée.
Il n'y aura faubourg, cité, ni ville,
Que par Babares pillée soit et volée.

From Monaco as far as Sicily
the whole coast will remain desolated.
There will be neither suburb, city nor
*   town*

that will not be pillaged and violated by
*   the Barbarians.* (II:4)

In the 16th century the 'Babares' inhabited the Mediterranean coast of North Africa and were distinguished mainly by their piratical skills, preying on the merchant ships of the region. This seems to be another quatrain that warns of the invasion of the West by poorer nations. Nostradamus implies that the devastation will be caused by pirates in search of booty, rather than by invaders who wish to conquer new lands.

Almost without exception, the *Prophecies* of Nostradamus deal with wars, intrigues, famines, plagues and the machinations of world leaders – there is little within the quatrains which could be described as being optimistic in outlook, or even neutral. He deals with life-threatening events, and presumably wrote them down in order to warn future generations. If Nostradamus really could look into the future, it opens up a new angle on the old debate about predestination and free will. It may not be within mankind's power to change its fate, but Nostradamus at least gives us a chance to prepare for it.

LEFT AND FAR LEFT: *A large toxic waste dump (left) symbolizes the profligacy of the western world. We produce more than we can consume, (and cannot even dispose of our waste safely) while the peoples of the third world starve. The near absence of the annual rains in Ethiopia regularly produces such scenes of misery.*

OVERLEAF: *A forest fire in Wyoming. The USA suffered from drought for several years in the late 1980s. A large part of the grain harvest was ruined and other areas suffered from devastating forest fires like this one. It would be ironic if Nostradamus's direst predictions for mankind were fulfilled simply by a change in the weather.*

ACKNOWLEDGMENTS

The author and publisher would like to thank the following for their help
in the production of this book: Elizabeth Montgomery for picture
research, Ron Watson for the index, and Design-23 for designing it. We
are also grateful to the following individuals and institutions for use of the
illustrations on the pages noted below.

Art Resource/Snark International 1,
The Bettmann Archive pp 4, 8(top), 9(bottom), 10(top right and
 bottom right), 11(both), 13(top), 16(below), 18(both), 19(both), 22,
 23(both), 24(bottom right), 25(all 3), 26(top), 28(bottom), 29(top),
 30(top), 44(bottom), 57(below), 58(both), 61, 71
Bundesarchiv pp 5(left and right), 37(bottom), 38(top right), 39(bottom)
Bison Picture Library pp 3(right), 13, 33(below), 34(both), 35, 36,
 38(bottom), 41(top left and bottom), 45(both), 65(both)
Peter Clayton 16(top left)
M. Doolittle/Rainbow 74(bottom)
European News and Features Ltd./Daily Express 38 (top left)
By permission of the Houghton Library, Harvard University
 8(bottom left and right)
Imperial War Museum 40(both)
Musée du Louvre, Paris/Art Resource(Scala) 15
Dan McCoy/Rainbow pp 3(center), 69(top), 70(bottom left)
Hank Morgan/Rainbow 69(bottom)
Musée Conde, Chantilly (Giraudon/Art Resource, NY) 9(top)
Musée de Salon et de la Crau, Salon de Provence pp 6(photo A.
 Vaillat), 7 and 13(bottom), photos Christian Breton
Museo Medici, Florence (Giraudon/Art Resource) 10(top left)
N.A.S.A. 70(top)
National Army Museum, London 16(bottom)
National Maritime Museum, London 12(top)
National Portrait Gallery, London 29(bottom)
Novosti 27(both)
Dario Poli pp 2, 14, 20, 32, 42, 56, 66
Reuters/Bettmann pp 3(left), 5(center), 43(below), 48, 49, 50(both),
 51(bottom), 52, 53, 54, 55(both), 59, 62(top), 67, 68(both), 72, 74(top),
 75, 76, 77
UPI/Bettmann pp 12(bottom), 37(top), 44(top), 46(top), 47, 51(top), 59,
 60, 62(bottom), 63(both), 64, 73(both), 78
U.S. Air Force pp 39(top), 41(top right)
Versailles, Chateau (Giraudon/Art Resource) pp 24(both), 28(top)
Victoria and Albert Museum, London 30(bottom)

AUTHOR'S NOTE

The French text reproduced is a partially modernized version of the
original 1568 edition of the *Prophecies*. The translations are the work of the
author.
The bibliography that follows is a small selection of the vast body of work
on Nostradamus and his predictions.
Cheetham, Erika, *The Final Prophecies of Nostradamus*, Futura 1989
de Fontbrune, Jean-Charles, *Nostradamus I: Countdown to Apocalypse*
Laver, James, *Nostradamus or the Future Foretold*
Leoni, Edgar, *Nostradamus: life and literature*
Ward, Charles A., *Oracles of Nostradamus*